What Now?

A Road Map for 80-Year-Olds and Beyond

Ronda Chervin, Ph.D.

Professor of Philosophy

and

Albert Hughes, Lt Colonel United States Air Force, Pastoral Counselor and Spiritual Director

En Route Books & Media, LLC
St. Louis, MO

⊕ *ENROUTE*
Make the time

En Route Books and Media, LLC
5705 Rhodes Avenue
St. Louis, MO 63109

Cover credit: TJ Burdick

Library of Congress Control Number:
2019948479

ISBN-13: 978-1-950108-36-7
ISBN-10: 1-950108-36-8

DEDICATION

To the Quiet Generation who soldier on.

Contents

Introduction

Ronda Chervin

"Our span is seventy years, or eighty for those who are strong." (Psalm 90)

The purpose of this roadmap is to provide Christian insight and inspiration to those 80 years or older. May it be a help to you on your 80-plus journey.

Until I reached the age of 80, I thought that there was no need for such insight and inspiration at such a time in life. I pictured myself a shut-in living in a bed, heavily sedated with pain killers, but with my soul soaring into eternity!

However, now at 82, happening to know still highly functioning 90-year-olds, I realize it isn't quite so simple.

What now? A Roadmap for 80-Year-olds and Beyond began, really, when I started inserting insights and inspirations into my Good Books Media blog (see goodbooksmedia.com for Ronda-View), which I am now doing on WCAT Radio (see https://wcatradio.com/ronda chervinsradiojournal/ for a show called Ronda Chervin's Radio Journal.

Develop the themes of the blog into a book? Well, I did write just such a book when I was 60 years old, entitled *Meeting Christ in the Joys and Sufferings of Aging*. But 60 is nothing like 80!

Talking about the idea of such a book for the 80-plus with Al Hughes, I was impressed that he came up with book and chapter titles immediately.

We had recently finished writing two books together: *Escaping Anxiety along the Road to Spiritual Joy* as well as *Simple Holiness: A Six-Week Walk on the Mountain of God;* both published by En Route Books and Media.

"Why don't you write it with me?" I begged. After all, you are pushing 80, too!"

He said, "Yes."

Now, I want to make it very clear that *What Now? A Roadmap for 80-Year-olds and Beyond* is not a professional geriatric book designed to help the elderly or their caretakers with the most agonizing problems we may be facing. So please do not take our small book as unsympathetic if, indeed, you are a reader suffering in those ways. We pray that you may find the help you need from Divine grace directly or through others whom God sends.

We are offering our book to you because we have been told these insights are of help.

As I begin writing *What Now? A Roadmap for 80-Year-Olds and Beyond,* here is my life-situation. I am alone, a widow dedicated to Christ, residing in a beautiful apartment on the Bay of Corpus Christi, Texas.

Retired! This is after eight years at Holy Apostles College and Seminary in Cromwell, Connecticut, where I taught philosophy and spirituality, and where I saw a hundred people every day at the 3 meals provided in the cafeteria.

I retired just before my 80th birthday. I would surely, finally, become a true contemplative and even, if God so willed, a Catholic mystic, levitating to the ceiling of the Church.

Instead, after a year-and-a-half of living alone, even though Jesus speaks to me in my heart, I find myself lonely and restless. "Me, myself, and I" are not my favorite human company!

Every day, I go to Holy Mass, spend an hour in silent prayer, recite the rosary, read the Liturgy of the Hours, and chat on my family's Facebook. Some days of each week I volunteer at the parish office, teach a few small groups, visit with my spiritual director, Al Hughes, and other friends. But still there are hours and hours of time with nothing to do!

Why not work on one final book?

Before going on to Al's introduction, I think it would be good for me to call to mind some of the good "models" I have of 80-year-olds among my family and friends.

My father, who died in his late 80's, was still writing up to the last 5 years of his life. Ralph De Sola was the author of many books, the most important of which was the standard Abbreviations Dictionary, updated every few years, available in public libraries.

He owned a beautiful house in San Diego, CA, with Spanish-American decor and large maps and pictures on the walls. Since he hated seeing relatives and friends fighting over legacies after people's deaths, he devised this helpful custom. For years before his death, when anyone came to visit he asked them which of the pictures, furniture, and books they wanted the most. Then he appended to these selections the name of the person they would be given to after his death by his executor. It worked. No fights.

When my mother Helen Winner De Sola, who was separated from my father in their 50's, turned 80 she had already made a transition from apartment living to a beautiful assisted living apartment building in Los Angeles overlooking the Pacific Ocean. But, then, due to greater dementia, she moved into a convalescent home, and finally to a room in our house with a live-in attendant.

Looking back, I realize she is a model for me of prudence in that she saved enough money from various editing jobs and social security to be able to live in such lovely surroundings at the end of her life.

She also was a model of humor and courage. Examples of humor: in the hospital after her colon cancer surgery, I came to visit her and tremulously asked her how she felt. "Well, the nurses aren't

very interesting to talk to!" she re-
marked; characteristic of her being such
a conversationalist all her life.

Another incident I will never forget is
the humor of my mother in a wheelchair
in our living room, bumping into the
stroller of my granddaughter.

"How do you like your first grand-
daughter?" I asked her.

"We have a lot in common. We're both
bored to death here!"

But the most wonderful part was the
last months of her life when she was on a
feeding tube. The Medicare group that
sent out attendants chose for her a
Filipino nurse who had trained under
Mother Teresa of Calcutta's Sisters.

Instead of focusing on my mother's
hygienic needs, she sat by her side all day
leading Mom in childish charismatic
songs of a type that, before this, my
mother would have scorned as senti-
mental drivel. So, I would find them
clapping their hands and singing: "Now

we're going to go to our Father's house where's there's joy, joy, joy!"

The aspect of my mother's '80s that impresses me the most is that even in the last year she could still exhibit the good personality traits that were always there, such as prudence and humor. And, that God could find some absolutely unpredictable way to reach us even on our death-beds.

I like to think of the account that my old friend, Alice Von Hildebrand, gives of the deathbed incidents of her famous husband, Dietrich Von Hildebrand. "As he lay dying, he prayed over and over again, 'Christ, bid me come unto Thee!'"

It seemed to me so touching that this renowned Catholic philosopher, at the end of his life, had only one wish; not to enunciate an unforgettable truth, but to beg our personal Savior to come to him.

My godmother, Leni Schwarz, was a loving, very helping woman, but she was also tense and easily upset when frustrated. It was a marvel to me to hear that when she was finally in a convalescent home with no duties, she became radiantly peaceful.

Myself a loving, but also very tense, easily irritated woman, I thought that possibly I finally would become peaceful when I had nothing to do but pray and praise.

Another 80-year-old: when I was in my late '60's, after Holy Mass friends used to bring me sometimes to visit this old, old, woman who lived on the same street as the Church. Although pretty much a shut-in, she was always beaming with joy. "She has a grateful heart," were the words a friend used to explain it!

I find that any day I devote to thanksgiving for every good thing in my life, all the way down to toilet paper, is a day that is joyful.

When I was a new convert in my early 20s, I was brought to see another old, holy woman. Her name was Marguerite Solbrig. She was the founder of a lay community. I only saw her for ten minutes. There was a bed with covers and all I could see was the face of this woman. Her large brown eyes were glowing with mingled suffering and joy as she looked at me with love.

I will never forget that look.

Now, at an age closer to hers, I am thinking: We shouldn't think that our life on earth is over if we can't do our usual work in the world or in the Church. With one look of love, if we truly live in the depth of the heart of Jesus, we could do something intensely meaningful for another person.

Al Hughes

"Life begins at 80," so I have heard. I wonder if those with such optimism had actually reached 80! Easy it is to assume, passing 60 or 70, that 80 is more of the same. It isn't. Now pushing 80 myself, I find myself in a new transition of a different sort. I can still do all that I could do at 65, but just less of it.

Add to that, oversight due to a forgetful short-term memory. (Did I take my pills? Is this Saturday?) Still, I can remember in detail the exact words expressed by my mother and I in a discrete conversation we had in the dining room when I was 15. I also have a single clear memory of the first time I was exposed to rabies. I was a 2-year-old, almost 3! Long term memory seems to be an increasing capability, which could be put to use, as in writing my autobiography at age 76.

And the need for extra care in staying balanced. In my motorcycle days, we used to say, "Keep the rubber side down!" Same principle now, but the rubber side is not tires, but the soles of my shoes. This is all new territory for me. I am older than any of my relatives and ancestors. None that I knew got past 74, except grandma "Gommie." She was pushing

103 when she made her last journey home.

But that was then, and this is now. Thanks to great leaps in medical technology, we are living longer. Much longer. When we were teens and twenties, folks were expected to retire at 65 and die at 67. So said the statistics. Thanks to a quad bypass at 65, the imminent, fatal heart attack I nearly experienced never happened.

Now, I play bridge mostly with folks in their '80s and '90s. Bob, a WWII fighter pilot, is 97 and still active. His wife is a vivacious young 91—a telephone operator during the same war. And I know a gal of 101 who has a walker; but seldom uses it. And another gal, now 101, who was a bomber pilot in WWII. She shuttled four engine bombers: B-17 flying fortresses, B-24s, B-29 Superfortresses and smaller combat aircraft from factories to air bases.

In various ways, the challenge they all have met is to remain active and relevant within their community as long as possible, despite the natural decline that takes place. The activities they pursue are normal, but they have mastered the transition required to mitigate declining strength and the entrenched cultural attitudes which tend to dismiss the elderly.

And that, in part, is the reason for this book! Cultural attitudes and accommodations regarding the elderly have not kept up with the realities of extended life expectation. Two examples:

A middle manager reaches age 55. Upper management appreciates his good work; but can hire two young workers for the same cost. Guess who gets laid off or is encouraged to leave? Inadvertently, the government encourages this activity at 55 through tax incentives. Unintended consequences.

A more natural process is a younger adult's growing disinterest and tendency to dismiss older persons. Often, the young, immersed in their own experience of life, cannot relate; or won't take the time to relate to the experiences of their elders; they don't want to hear our stories.

For such reasons, among many others, we have decided to offer understandings and coping strategies for the elderly, that we elders may succeed in life's final challenges.

For Personal Reflection and Group Sharing

- What is your present life-situation?

- Do you have any good "models" of 80-year-olds you admired?

What Were the Dreams for My Life?

"In the last days, God says, I will pour out my Spirit on all people. Your sons and daughters will prophesy, your young men will see visions, your old men will dream dreams." (Acts 2, 17)

by Ronda

When I thought about this question I was surprised to find that none of my dreams, at any time of my life, came true! But God brought about good things that I could never have dreamed of, as you will see.

As a schoolgirl, my dream was to fit in with the popular kids. I couldn't.

Why not?

Because most of them were upper-middle-class Jewish families whose fathers were businessmen. Not ex-Communist, highly literary lower-middle-class parents like mine. I didn't dress like them; I didn't talk like them; and I didn't live in a big apartment with fancy furniture.

Instead, gradually I became a kind of leader of others who didn't fit in.

Looking back, I am interested to notice that my twin-sister didn't seem to have that dream of fitting in! She dreamed of becoming a dancer. And she did!

As a teenager, I dreamed of becoming a femme fatale, along the lines of Scarlett O'Hara in *Gone with the Wind*. I couldn't.

Why not?

I was small-busted; pretty, but not sexy.

Instead, I dated far-out types – mad geniuses - what would now be called "nerds."

Looking back, I am interested to notice that my twin-sister didn't seem to dream of becoming a femme fatale. She dreamed of becoming a beautiful soloist. And she did!

In my 20s, after becoming a Catholic, I dreamed of marrying a man like St. Francis of Assisi. I couldn't.

Why not?

Because men like that become Franciscans!

Instead, I married an atheist of Jewish orthodox lineage who was a divorced play-boy! We got a dispensation from his first marriage, and he eventually became a Catholic. We had a wonderful marriage in spite of severe conflicts.

Looking back, I am interested to note that my twin-sister, also a convert to the Catholic faith, didn't hunt frantically for perfect husbands and, in some ways, her marriage was more harmonious than mine!

I dreamed of having a large Catholic family—maybe 13 children all who would be as saintly as the ones of the parents of St. Therese of Lisieux. I couldn't.

Why not?

After having twin girls, I had 3 miscarriages; and after having a son, I had 3 more miscarriages!

However, as was the case with my twin-sister, we both became teachers with many, many students who viewed us as inspiring mother figures.

As a Catholic, I read the lives of the saints and mystics. I dreamed that one day I would be a holy mystic, going into trances in prayer and levitating on the ceiling and with a large following. I couldn't.

Why not?

Because God called me instead to be a philosophy professor, a speaker, and a writer. And, over decades, many say that I influenced them for the good.

My twin-sister didn't dream of such graces. Instead she cultivated silent prayer and developed sacred dance in the Church. Her maiden name, used in her dance, is Carla De Sola. You can google her YouTubes to see how beautiful this is.

I was 57 when my husband died. I dreamed of marrying a second husband who would be a saint. I couldn't.

Why not?

Because the single men I had in mind didn't want to marry me. It took me a while to figure out that if a 70-year-old man had never married, it wasn't just because he never met me!

Instead, God led me to the vocation of "dedicated widow," a widow who makes a private promise not to re-marry and live for Jesus as her second bridegroom; to serve in the Church.

My twin-sister didn't dream of second husbands after her husband died, nor did she make such a widow promise, but she lives a life dedicated to the Church.

In the part in *What Now? A Roadmap for 80-Year-Olds and Beyond* that deals with trying to find the right living situation in old age, I will tell you about my dreams of a community of aging literary, intellectual, creative Catholics.

Guess what? It hasn't happened!

And, having traced this history of my dreams, I figure, again, God will do something else wonderful for me instead.

by Al

When I was young, I had many and varied ideas about who I might become, but I don't grant them the status of "dreams." They were casual ideas in response to passing events. I remember thinking about being a railroad engineer, an astronomer, a builder of telescopes, a musician, a mathematician, an artist, a teacher – I don't know, maybe others: a doctor, a lawyer, an Indian chief; even a vagabond, a wanderer. So, I would like to take a different approach than Ronda's by identifying clues I remember that indicated what I actually would become.

Ronda's humorous account of her failed dreams reveals a profound reality.

Regardless of our dreams, we have received God-given purposes. We are equipped to carry out God's plan, not ours. Final failure in life would indicate plans not found or God's plans rejected. As my beloved wife used to say, "God has a plan for everyone, God has a plan."

Child prodigies seem born knowing their plan; others never find theirs or never try to discern it. But most seem to work it out along the way. Have you figured out God's plan for yourself? Ronda was born to be a thinker. She found that out at 30. I was born to manage and command teams of professional specialists, later to become a teacher-evangelist, a spiritual director, and an author. If you have not discovered your plan – the 80's, even 90's yet may reveal what you still might accomplish. Even if only in your own community or household.

As for me, there were clues from early childhood, "decoded" in my senior year of college. The basic principle in determining God's plan for us all was stated by Bishop Z____ at a retreat I attended maybe 30 years ago. He said, "If you love the work you do, it's your work. If you hate your work, it is someone else's work." That is your primary indicator. What do you love doing? Get after it at any age to the best of your ability and circumstance. It is your plan in God's realm.

Here is my example, with early clues indicating who I would become. Study it, then search your memory for clues to what your plan was in God.

I was first treated for rabies at the ripe old age of 2! I only tell you this as an introduction to the second time I was treated for rabies. The first time, I was licked all over my face: mouth, nose, eyes, ears. I remember that friendly farm dog who showed up with rabies symptoms two days later, but I do not remember the shots.

The second occasion at age 5 was much worse. A dog attacked me and chewed on my face. The next day he was found dead of rabies in a woodlot across the street. I had a violent reaction to the rabies serum this time and wound up in a polio clinic for 3 months. It was the only facility that could continue my rabies treatment with any hope of success.

The clue to God's plan for me? I remember organizing and leading war games in our ward when the nurses were occupied down the hall; artillery duels bed-to-bed with rubber bands and paper wads among a dozen 5-year-old boys who still could move about despite their polio infirmities. The kids in the iron lungs only could listen to the bedlam.

At 8, our family attended a symphony concert. At intermission, my mother asked which instrument I would like to play. I thought about that a moment and said, "I want to be the guy with the stick!" That is to say, the conductor, the boss, the commander.

Early in my senior year of high school I suddenly emerged as the class leader after years of obscurity. With my girl-friend, I was co-editor on the school newspaper, *The Grit*; president of the Civics club, etc., and I taught the senior trigonometry course since no qualified high school teacher was available.

The leadership clues were there but unrecognized until my senior year in college. I had to take one more elective. I signed up for a course entitled "Intro-duction to Management." Had no clue what it was about, but I had to take one more elective.

I bought the text by the same title, took it back to the dorm and started to read. Before I finished the introduction to the book, I knew who I was. The introduction alone was thrilling to me, and every chapter renewed the thrill. I was to be a professional manager.

Did I dream of a wife and children? No. I was self-sworn to be a lifetime bachelor. But God *did* have a dream for me. Her name is Jeannie.

For Personal Reflection and Group Sharing:

- Do you remember your dreams for your life?

- Can you find good that came in your life that you wouldn't have dreamed of – part of God's plan for you?

Where did I succeed?

"Well done good and faithful servant. You have been faithful in little things. I will put you in charge of many things." (Matthew 25:21)

by Ronda

Note to reader: As you hear about the successes of we the authors of this book, you may find that your successes are much greater than ours, or you might think that your successes are not as important. For example, when we were reading our original version of this chapter to some friends, it seemed as if they didn't like reading in detail about all our accomplishments.

But consider that a construction worker who has contributed to some 50 homes and/or 5 bridges is a big success in his/her own field. Or, a housewife who kept the residence clean with children messing it up every day is successful in that, even though it wouldn't make an item in a resume!

And, after all, to have gotten to 80 years of age is itself a success!

Our intent is not that you compare your successes to ours. The purpose of this chapter is to help you to think about all the positives in your past. Later, we will be dealing with our seeming failures. You shouldn't be thinking you have no successes because they are not newsworthy. "She never wrote a book, she never made a movie, little known beyond her village, but she was the mother of Jesus."

Another point can be made here about humility. Truth is that everything we do that is good is with God's grace. Our life and all our talents are his gifts. What we are doing is presenting a model for you to follow in recalling your own successes.

So, on to my thoughts about my successes.

Often, I speak at Catholic Conferences. There I enjoy meeting other speakers and writers and chatting at the dinner table with them.

Here is a conversation I never will forget:

Scott Hahn: "Ronda, don't you hate the adulation?"

After a short pause:

Ronda: "No, Scott, the adulation is the only thing that keeps me going!"

However, because we know, as believers in the Creator God, that everything we have that is good is a gift from God, we are admonished never to act proud of our own talents, as if we had invented them, or to consider any success of ours to come simply a result of our own efforts.

If we are true believers, we surely very often pray for the Holy Spirit to help us with our endeavors, and surely we thank God when things go well.

Sometimes, when a lovely praise-filled introduction about my accomplishments is presented to an audience, I smile and say something like this:

"Hearing all this, you may be envying me. But if you could live in my head for a month, you would never envy me!"

And when a woman comes up to me after a talk and modestly says something like:

"I wanted to tell you something, but I'm only a housewife..."

I ask her how many children she has.

"Four."

"And which of those children, who will hopefully live for an eternity in heaven, would you exchange for writing a book that will one day disintegrate in a garbage can?"

Another favorite saying of mine to fans is "I am only good at speaking and writing, you should see me in daily life trying to cook, or drive, or clean!"

That said, when I look back over my 80 years of life, I do consider that, with the grace of God, I have succeeded, for the most part, as a Catholic philosophy teacher, speaker, and writer.

It gives me enormous joy when I get e-mails from students from decades ago saying how my classes helped them; or how some one sentence in a talk changed their lives, or how they cherish a book I wrote some 50 years ago.

These occupations brought me sufficient income to live on and support my family after my husband became disabled with asthma 5 years into our marriage. I consider that to be financial success.

However, most readers do not know that the profits from the sale of books largely are divided between the publisher and the bookstore. Authors used to get 6% of sales, and now 10%. So, when you see a writer laying out books on the table at a conference and urging you to look for something you want, it is not because of profit, unless the speaker commands best-selling sales around the world, like Stephen King. It is because we put so much work and prayer into them that we really want to see readers benefit.

Also, I consider it a great success to have passed the torch of my very personalistic ways of teaching to students of mine who became teachers themselves. And, also, to have encouraged many writers to persevere and get their works published.

And, so, I end these accounts with this prayer:

God, the Father, thank you for the gift of philosophical reasoning and the truths it gave me. Thank you for the gift of articulating truth as a teacher and speaker and writer. Please expunge from the minds of any of my listeners or readers anything that was not true, or only half-true. May anything I say or write in the last years of my life be inspired by the Holy Spirit for the building of Your kingdom.

Another area I see as success is winning fantastic friends, of course, as gifts of God.

Now, I don't consider a friend to be someone I happen to like, but whom I even might not remember after I move away. I am thinking of friends whose love I cherish because they have seen me at my worst and still hang-in!

When Al and I were working on our book *Escaping Anxiety along the Road to Spiritual Joy,* he asked me to heal my memories by making a list of all those people whom I thought really loved me in my whole 80 years of life.

I came up with 48 in about half an hour!!!!

Again, let me thank You, Father God, for this incredible gift!

by Al

I have divided my successes into three categories: intellectual, professional, and other. Some only have to be listed; others may beg a short explanation. You will select your own format if you choose to list your successes.

Collegiate Successes

Bachelor of Science; Master of Science; Master of Pastoral Ministry; Master of Arts (equivalent) in Spiritual Direction.

Professional Successes

21-year successful career in the United States Air Force; 12 years success as a Department manager at ITT Federal Services.

My command of Antigua Air Station, Antigua Island, West Indies, was particularly interesting, as diplomacy was part of the job. My working relationships included the British Governor, the Antigua Premier and cabinet ministers, the British government representative, the US Ambassador down south at Barbados Island, and a constant parade of admirals, generals and English knights. Some of those from off island were overnight house guests. See my book *Paradise Commander* (to find it quickly, go to Goodbooksmedia.com.)

Retired in the permanent rank of Lt. Colonel, USAF, regular line officer.

Other Successes

Catholic catechist, retreat master; founded, directed and taught the Rite of Christian Initiation for Adults (RCIA) at Santa Maria, CA. Also taught RCIA in Corpus Christi, TX, completing 25 years.

Spiritual Director Last 24 years. Dean, Our Lady of Corpus Christi

Author, *Paradise Commander; Saint Jeannie's Shiny Black Shoes; Buddy, Can You Spare a (para) 'Digm; Why I am Still a Catholic* (all obtainable from Goodbooksmedia.com.) Also, with co-author Ronda Chervin, PhD, *Escaping Anxiety Along the Road to Spiritual Joy; Simple Holiness, a Six Week Walk on the Mountain of God.* Finally, my autobiography, *Ice Fog, Spirit Fire and the Narrow Gate* (all obtainable from Enroutebooksandmedia.com).

48-year sacramental marriage to a living saint (seriously!), who is now deceased.

Blue water ocean sailor: Chesapeake Bay, coast of Florida, trans-Bahamas, Daytona to Bermuda race, central and eastern Caribbean.

My favorite memories?

Senior director, Space Defense Center, Antigua Air Station Command, husband, author. Being at the helm of a 45-ft. cruising catamaran surfing the big, heavy boat down the face of 10-foot waves at sunset; while departing west out of San Salvador Island, Bahamas.

For Personal Reflection and Group Sharing:

- What do you think of as your successes? (Not only professional, but in every aspect of life.)

- As you go along writing your own successes down or remembering them in your mind, you might thank God for the talents He gave you and the help along the way.

Where did I fail?

"For the righteous falls 7 times and rises again." (Proverbs 24:16)

by Ronda

I find that the sense of having failed can be a trap, especially in retrospective analysis of one's life. For example, I usually share a lot about the sad things in my marriage, mostly to convince people of how important forgiveness is.

But, once a priest said this: "Stop talking about how you had a bad marriage. Did you help your husband get to heaven?"

"Oh, sure. After all, he might never have become a Catholic if he didn't marry me and, by the end of his life he was a daily Mass Catholic going to Church with me every morning."

"So, then, you had a very successful marriage!" the priest insisted.

I find that many 80-year-olds and beyond are grieved deeply by what we consider to be our failure to pass on to all of our children the thing we valued most: our Catholic faith.

Perhaps before you leave this world, or from purgatory or heaven you will witness those beloved adult children turning to Jesus with all their hearts, also back in the sacraments!

In the journal of my son when he committed suicide at age 19 amidst accounts of terrible bouts with demonic thoughts, I found the words in big letters "JESUS, SAVE ME!"

(You can find more about my marriage in my autobiography: *En Route to Eternity* (Miriam Press), and more about my son's death in *Weeping with Jesus: From Grief to Hope* (En Route Books and Media).

Here in this book *What Now? A Roadmap for 80-year-olds and Beyond,* I want to write about my failures as a wife and mother from an 80-year-old's perspective.

Not all, but probably most of other old women I talk to who were wives and mothers came from Catholic families with a lot of good models for these roles. The fact that my parents weren't married at all, separated when my twin sister and I were 8 years old, and that we had no younger brothers and sisters, contributed to my truly unusual lack of experience coming to marriage and parenting.

Looking back on 33 years of marriage, now as a widow of 23 years, my diagnosis of the problems is very different than when I was immersed in those roles. I now think that the biggest failure was in communication and in forgiveness.

It astounds me that a woman and a man as articulate as Martin and I both were spent so little time talking about the roots of our disappointments in each other. How I wish we had gone to marriage counseling instead of spending years in "quiet desperation," fighting over conflicts that came out of each other's negative traits!

The grace of unconditional mutual forgiveness came only in the last decade of our marriage.

When talking to married couples, I like to encapsulate what I learned from our journey in these words:

First the spouse can be an idol; then a fallen idol; but, then, after real, deep, forgiveness we could laugh at the same things that enraged us in each other and see each other more like funny little creatures!

When my twins were born 9 months after our marriage, it was only the second time in my life I had ever even touched a baby! I loved, loved, loved the unique personalities of my little baby girls. I loved the charming cuteness of them. I loved the souls I could see reflected in their beautiful eyes.

But I hadn't a clue how to be a mother in practical terms. I relied heavily on Dr. Spock and passing advice of friendly mothers whom I met at the playground. By the time my darlings were a year and a half old they were running wildly around our apartment, and I was hiding behind the kiddie-gate in the kitchen trying to read up on disciplining toddlers!

I have never met any other mothers who were stuck in my mental problem: "If table manners aren't moral absolutes, how can I demand that the kiddies conform to them?"

If success in parenting is measured by obedience of the children, then I was certainly a failure.

However, what I was able to give them was certainly also important: a spirit of praise of God for the beauty of nature, the gift of communication through words to match every experience of their lives, and hearts full of love for their own children.

And, even though, at this writing, though brought up Catholic, they are not into the sacraments of the Church, they are close to God in their hearts.

I notice in my own thinking, and also that of other parents of adult children, that we sometimes sound as if our children were our products and their shortcomings are, therefore, a sign that we failed in making a perfect product.

But that is a flawed idea. Surely children are free-will creatures of God who make their own good and bad decisions. It is a form of pride to attribute to ourselves all their virtues and negatively to blame ourselves totally for all their faults.

Jesus seems to tell me about my children: "You didn't create them; I did. You can't save them. I can."

Here is my prayer: Dear Jesus, please compensate my husband on his journey in eternity for all my harsh judgments and non-forgiveness. And may he, and our son, intercede for our daughters as they make their way into Your arms. Forever together some day!

Now, this chapter would not be complete if I left out a big area of failure. What is it? Trying to become holy!

The French novelist Leon Bloy coined this famous saying: "There is only one tragedy in life: not to have become a saint!"

I do believe, humorously perhaps, that I've got to make purgatory because I try so hard, but that is not the same as, after death, soaring to God freed of not only sin but all the consequences of sin.

Now, just so you, the reader, don't immediately think: "Oh, Ronda is just a scrupulous wretch, we all know she is holy!" I will explain clearly why I am not, by my own definition.

I define holiness in my book *The Way of Love* as having nothing but love in one's heart: joyful love, grateful love, sorrowing love, anguished love...but absolutely not having pockets of the wrong kind of anger, trustless anxiety, despair, disgruntlement, or even the blahs!

Now I am not so bad at blahs because I am a highly energetic person, bubbling over with projects, and I rarely am even tempted to despair, but the other negatives...!

And so, I pray, Jesus, source of all graces of holiness, please forgive me for all that anger, anxiety, and disgruntlement. Thank you for bringing me wonderful spiritual mentors and friends who still try to liberate me from these syndromes. May Your love eradicate these syndromes before I leave this world.

by Al

"The sins of the father are visited upon the third generation." I think you will find that quote both in the Old Testament and the New. That always was and still is true. The ancients observed it as a reason for God to punish sons and grandsons. Jesus spoke against that understanding.

But it also applies to generational behaviors within families.

The behavior of one generation influences the following two generations (or more). Through cultural and psychological studies, we now know – at least in part – how that transgenerational behavior has worked in recent times.

There are two major causes operating in my life; but I do not use this knowledge of cause as an excuse. A sin still is a sin. If you prefer other language, a failure is still a failure.

The first cause started 200 years ago, the industrial revolution. It took fathers out of the house or the farm or the family shop where they used to work, relate to and teach their children manners, faith, work skills and cooperative attitudes. Opportunities for what we now call "quality time" began to wane due to the daily absence of fathers.

The second cause is genetics, analyzed by a recently maturing science. To a great extent, we are like our parents and grandparents (three generations, right?) We are related to them not only according to blood, but in various mixes by intellect, physical strength, cultural behavior, susceptibility to illness, and more.

My own significant failures are the failures of a host of other men in our time, leading often to failures on a societal scale. As for me personally, during the early and teen years of my children, I was so entrenched in the life of an Air Force officer, absent much of each day and sometimes for a week or more on temporary duty elsewhere around the nation, that quality time was nearly impossible. Add to that prevalent cultural attitudes which seem a spillover from my preceding two generations that "I will take care of earning sufficient money for my family. Raising the kids is my wife's job." That attitude effectively assures and tries to justify the absence of quality time.

As for me, you also can add in that it was a case of a certain mental deficiency, despite my intelligence. It came upon me so slowly that for years I thought I was just too tired to deal with the kids. But about age 50 I was diagnosed with clinical depression, a slowly increasing deficiency of certain chemicals necessary for proper brain function. Once found, it took just a month to cure.

Once I understood my own symptoms experientially, I soon realized my father and my paternal grandfather had the same symptoms! (They also evidenced the same failings as I, the lack of quality time with their children). 'The sins" (faults if you prefer) of the father are visited upon the third generation of families because the causes extend over at least three generations.

The suffering I caused my two daughters (similar to my father's and my own childhood suffering) seems to have fallen primarily on my elder daughter. My diagnosis and cure came in time to minimize the effect on the younger, as upon the cure, my attention to the girls increased dramatically. It seemed as if it was just too late for my elder daughter. Rejection by many school mates also contributed. For instance, they ridiculed her gift for poetry.

Their mother did the best she could, but children need the guidance and warmth of both parents. Men and women *are* different, and each guides a child according to his/her own individual experience of life. Further, experiencing the remoteness of a parent, a child is likely to presume personal guilt or make a decision of non-worth.

My younger daughter escaped this fate and now is an accomplished Catholic evangelist and one of my best friends. The elder rebelled *in extremis* at the end of high school. However, eventually she did become a wife in a stable marriage.

Again, I repeat, knowledge of my contributing causes does not excuse the fault. My faulty behavior toward my children was based in my own decisions at the time, regardless.

For Personal Reflection and Group Sharing:

- What do you think of as failures in your life?

- Have you sought forgiveness for your failures?

Pain and Fear of Worse Pain

You have taken my friends away from me: you have made me hateful in their sight, I am shut in, I may not go out. My eyes are weak from my sufferings. I have called to you, Lord, all the day; I have stretched out my hands to you. (Psalm 88 (89)

by Ronda

For many years, I have taught about euthanasia in ethics classes at universities and seminaries. The issue usually revolves around the question of a person's so-called right to avoid physical pain when he or she deems that it is not worth it to continue living under such circumstances.

Although this question sometimes concerns younger people's decisions, on our pilgrim's roadmap for 80-year-olds and beyond, we will focus on pain in old age.

An aspect of the debate that I have found both confusing and important is the variations of pain tolerance that are relevant to solutions.

Here is a spectrum I have observed:

A woman friend of mine has had great pain, sometimes acute, but always present for 30 years in spite of the best medicines available. Asked if she was praying for death, since as a strong believer, she would expect to be united to Jesus in heaven sooner that way, she replied, unexpectedly, "Of course, not! Life is so beautiful."

Others consider that a relatively small amount of chronic daily pain is something to accept and would prefer such pain to any drug that would put them into a semi-comatose state where they couldn't enjoy all the things in life they still have.

These may be the majority of sufferers of pain who are over 80 years old.

By contrast, I am so intolerant of physical pain, that any amount more severe than a dull, chronic small amount of pain would cause me to pray for death and/or insist on pain-killers; even if the side-effects led me to be comatose in bed for the rest of my life.

Euthanasia, is defined in diction-ary.com/browse/euthanasia

"Also called mercy killing. the act of putting to death painlessly or allowing to die, as by withholding extreme medical measures, a person or animal suffering from an incurable, especially a painful, disease or condition."

Now, the Catholic Church teaches that it is intrinsically wrong actively to cause the death of an innocent person, even if that person requests such action because of pain. However, we are not obliged to use extreme measures to stay alive. And, in cases where there is no cure for our disease, we are allowed to take as much painkiller as we think we need, even if a side effect might be our death. The reasoning is, you are not willing your death, but wanting to be free of pain.

What constitutes an extreme measure can be controversial in individual cases, since extremity of pain is one factor along with exorbitant expense and other concerns.

Since extremity of pain coming from a procedure medically helpful varies with an individual patient's tolerance of pain, it is advised to give a medical power of attorney to a trusted person, to help make such decisions.

The crosses of physical pain for 80-year-olds and beyond can be heavy. And

fear of future painful conditions ca
a great deal of the emotional pain or
anxiety even for those without any pain
in the present.

Here are some ways I have found
helpful for dealing with physical and
emotional pain:

Pray for healing, in the form of
something like this: Jesus, I wish You
would lay your healing hand on me, as if
I were on the streets of Galilee. I wish you
would heal me, but I accept whatever you
permit to happen to me, no matter how
painful.

I give whatever amount of physical
pain I am experiencing to You, Jesus,
accepting Your permissive will, and unit-
ing it to Your pain on the cross; accepted
for the redemption of our sins.

Now, this is easier, of course, if it is a
type of pain I know is for a short time
only such as in a dental extraction when
a Novocain is not as effective as I thought
it would be. Another example would be
the much worse pain of labor in child-

birth when a massive pain-killing shot cannot be administered for some medical reason. But, again, in the back of her mind, the mother knows that it is temporary.

Since I have not experienced long-term acute or massively dull pain for any long period in my life, so far, I cannot give personal witness to what helps spiritually; but I can tell you about how others have been helped.

Some press a crucifix to their chest in the area of the heart and pray "Jesus, crucified, help me." (See Fr. Larry Tucker, SOLT – *The Prayer of Jesus Crucified* (En Route Books and Media, 2017).

Others breath in and out the word Jesus, or Abba Father, or some other short prayer until the emotional tension added to the physical pain subsides.

"Jesus, I trust in You," part of the Mercy Chaplet prayers, is a big help.

Offering up the pain for one's most heartfelt wishes is a very traditional

Catholic way to cope. The usual form would be something like "Jesus, I offer to you, all my pain, toward the salvation of everyone in my family." (Or whatever is uppermost in one's soul.)

Fear of total disability is a different subject. Someone could be disabled in a bed, or in a wheel-chair, limited to the home unless brought somewhere else by a care-taker, without being in much pain. Such problems will be dealt with in our chapter on Limitations of 80-year-olds and Beyond. There, we will include the specific subject of dementia, including Alzheimer's.

Here is my prayer: Jesus, I accept whatever pain you will allow in my life. Unite it with yours for the coming of Your kingdom. Take away the anxiety I have about worse pain in the future. Give wisdom to my doctors and nurses. Jesus, I trust in You.

by Al

With gratitude to Providence, I have not been sick for about a dozen years, except for a little allergy trouble. I cannot speak from recent experience about significant pain or fear of pain/ disability. But I can draw conclusions from pains long past. Conclusions that are independent of any particular age, still relevant.

First: psychological pain of rejection and loneliness. Already, I have mentioned the polio clinic. From there, I went straight into first grade. As you might imagine, after three months confined to bed, plus complications from near constant normal childhood illnesses, I was tiny, emaciated, weak. The class bullies were first to notice, followed by the first-grade jocks. Not knowing my recent history of illness, they would not allow me to participate in their games. Automatically, implicitly, I was deemed – or concluded, I was a social outcast. Their assumptions about me were carried over from grade to grade.

As children often do, I blamed myself and withdrew from discourse; believing myself to be unworthy. This recurred from time to time even into my young adulthood. Which only added to my emotional pain of isolation. The lesson for all ages? If you feel isolated or alone for any reason, do not add to your pain of isolation by accepting this as the way things are. Reach out to others to the best of your ability – not by complaining, but by cheerfully offering help, encourage-ment and sincere affirmation to others who well might be suffering some form of isolation or self-doubt, themselves.

Second: at nineteen I had an appen-dectomy. The appendix burst during the operation, adding a third week to my recovery. Someone gave me a book to read during the second week. Title? *May Your House Be Safe from Tigers*! It was so hilarious that I created my own pain, pulling on the stitches with deep belly laughs. But the residual constant pain from the operation quickly disappeared. Both my behavior and that of the author relieved his pain and mine by focusing on something other than the constant pain. He, the author, wrote that hilarious book while in great pain, dying of cancer!

Third: While a Captain in the Air Force, I began to suffer an extreme pain right at the base of my sternum. A terrible pain at the top of my stomach. From work at Hanscom AFB, I walked up the hill to the base hospital. They "turned me inside out;" all the technology of that time: EEG, EKG, blood tests, reflex tests, X-ray pictures, etc.

Finally, the lead doctor called me back to his office and said, "There is absolutely nothing wrong with you. How are things going at work?"

"Lousy," I said. "My prime contractor is killing my program with incompetence and I surly will get the blame!"

"That is your problem," he said. "Pure anxiety".

What Now?

On the way back down the hill I suddenly realized the pain was gone. Knowledge of the source cured the condition. I promised myself that never would I let work do that to me again. Got a new pain? Unresolved anxiety? You may want to read our recent book, *Escaping Anxiety Along the Road to Spiritual Joy*.

On the other hand, if you have a slight pain that is slowly getting worse, beware. Get it checked! I ignored a slight chest pain that slowly got worse over a year and a half while I ignored it. When I finally checked into the ER, the emergency room doctor told me that I was within a few minutes of a massive heart attack! (I am still here, thanks to a jiffy quick quad bypass!)

I also should mention my wife. She had Alzheimer's. Until the last night of her life, she had no physical pain whatever, just a steady decline in her speech capability. Knowing that she faced death, still she actually was joyous during her decline. I remember her dancing in the living room with our housekeeper (neither of us danced in our years together) and in the absence of the housekeeper, dancing with a pillow that had the face of the crucified Jesus on it. I still have that pillow. Two weeks before her death, finally bed ridden, she repeated again and again to the doctor and to me, "I just want to see Jesus." In that, she was fully conscious to the end. The lesson for all ages? A real, honest faith in Christ makes a world of difference!

Here is one story that has little to do with great pain, though it does have to do with my crew's mild suffering. I was in command of a tactical operations crew at a radar site in Alaska, monitoring Soviet missile launches. Half my crew had the unenviable job of watching TV screens that would indicate detection of a Soviet launch. They had to be conscious of any indication for eight straight hours.

Can you imagine watching a blank TV screen for eight hours on a midnight shift when the Soviets were apparently inactive? Nothing going on? One of the guys kept the crew awake in this way. He would lean back in his chair, quietly count the tiny holes in the acoustic tile and loudly announce the count just as the others started nodding.

Then he would go to the next tile and the next, and the next one. Each time loudly announcing the count as another crew member started to slip into dream land. He kept us laughing off and on all night. The lesson for all time and all ages? Don't concentrate on you pain! Keep your mind busy on something else.

As to fear of future pain, I can't contribute much. I simply don't. When I woke up from that quad bypass there was a nurse standing there with a cup of water and a couple of pills. I inquired. They were pain pills. I refused them and we had a big argument. She finally left in a huff saying I would be sorry, terrible pains were on the way.

In my case not so. I was out of there in nine days with nary a pain. Three months later I was visiting a friend in the same hospital. Recognized a male nurse who had been there when I was in recovery. I walked over and started to introduce myself. He stopped me, saying, "I know who you are. We are still talking about you!" Miracles do happen!

For Personal Reflection and Group Sharing:

- Describe your own struggles with pain in the past and, especially, in the present.

- What are spiritual means that have helped you in dealing with pain?

Left Behind by Loved Persons Dying First

"We do not want you to be unin-formed about those who sleep in death... so that you will not grieve like the rest who have no hope." (1 Thessalonians 4:13)

by Ronda

Before the suicide of my son and the death of my husband I had a very limited knowledge of the grieving process. I thought that when someone who I loved would die, I would go through a few weeks of loud, weeping grief and then I would go on with my life!!!

I would guess that most readers over 80 and beyond would say that the loss of beloved persons has been the worst suffering of their lives.

A therapist told me after the suicide of my son, in 1991, that the process of the diminishing of grief is so very slow that we can hardly see that it is happening. In fact, though, most of us go from acute grief felt all day and through the night when awake, to every 5 minutes another wave of acute sorrow, and then gradually over time to several times a day but not constant and...less and less. After a year or so, it becomes a kind of dull ache. It never wholly goes away in this life. I think of it as like the swords in Mother Mary's heart shown in paintings of her. But even 20 years afterwards we suddenly can be convulsed with tearful grief by some association such as the birthday of that loved one.

I have chronicled my grief over my son, Charles Chervin, in my book *Weeping with Jesus: from Grief to Hope,* published by En Route Books and Media. It also includes chapters about proofs for the immorality of the soul helpful to those thrown into doubt when a loved one dies.

The story of my own feelings and those of widow-saints, I wrote about in great detail in my book *Walk with me, Jesus: A Widow's Journey*. Since I don't think there is any other book that reveals how the widow-saints went through grief and how they went on their holy journeys afterwards, I highly recommend it. It is published by Simon Peter Press, part of Women of Grace. You can just google the title to find it.

That is not to say that there are no good aspects to the death of loved ones. Of course, first of all there is the gratitude for having known that loved person. I often ask myself whether I would forfeit that love just to avoid the suffering of being with them in their dying process and the loss afterwards.

On the humorous side, I like to quip in talks to married couples, "the result of losing a spouse is that you realize that the absence of annoyance is not joy"!

A deeper way of explaining this is that when we are no longer the victim of the faults of the spouse, we will miss all their virtues much more!

A lesser form of grieving takes place when close, close friends leave this world. We miss everything we loved about them from how kind they were to us all the way to how they made us laugh. We also miss having someone around who has known us sometimes for our whole long lives – remembering us as kids, remembering our now adult children as babies.

I find a great consolation in looking at photos of beloved dead. I paid a techie grandson to put all my favorites of such photos up on the screen-saver of my computer where they rotate around all day. Since mostly people are smiling when on camera, I always can remember them not when they scowled at me, but when their faces were full of joy and love.

Another big help in all the losses of loved ones, family and friends, is to picture their resurrected bodies someday in heaven with us, assuming, hopefully that, through repentance, they make it into purgatory.

More about that in later chapters of *Roadmap...*

by Al

Grandpas Hughes and Salter; grandmas Hughes and Salter, uncles Salter and Green, aunt Green, cousin Howard. I knew these all and when I was very young they were a part of my life. But by their deaths, they were remote entities to me. We had moved out of middle Mississippi after WWII, and most of them who lived there died while I was on active duty; perhaps in Alaska, or the Caribbean or Cape Canaveral or Seattle, etc. Their deaths caused little or no emotional reaction.

But then, I am a strong intellectual thinker, not a feeler like my wife. She readily responded in a feeling way, but as she often said to me early in our marriage, "You are as cold as a fish!" It is not that I don't have feelings as she initially thought, but that feelings are not prominent in my psyche. When they pop up I quickly suppress or simply ignore them.

But then, my father died. I got the call on my console during the midnight shift. I was a Senior Director in the Space Defense Center. My mother was crying. It was about two am. Immediately, I informed my second on crew and the Command Director. I thanked Colonel Throckmorton but declined his offer that I stand down. I was sitting at an apex of the most capable communications system in the country.

Instead, I called back to the NORAD operator who had put the call through to my console. She knew my dad had died and expected me. We went to work, patching in to airline emergency desks. At that late hour the best they could do was fly me to Fort Worth, remain overnight, then fly on to Lafayette, La., the closest airport to home.

That night in an airport hotel was terrible. My father was unchurched and so was I back then, yet I feared for him and – I feared for me. It made me focus on the fact of death, with no comfort of understanding. My feelings that night were extreme and there was no work or responsibility or activity to distract me from awful thoughts through the night.

My mother's death, about ten years later, was expected. Lung cancer. The original diagnosis gave her six months, but she got two more good years before she crashed. I was there at her side. In my youth she had been my mentor and my champion. I owe much of my present life and success to her example and en-couragement. But unlike with my father's death, my feelings were muted. In this case, death was expected, and a quick death terminated the suffering of a slow drowning for lack of oxygen.

Finally, my wife died three years ago. Alzheimer's. But this was very different. By then we both had lived a solid Christian life, had shared in the Pentecostal experience, had vowed unconditional obedience to God, and God had directed our lives into a long avocational career as evangelists. Her death, I have already written above, was joyful, except for the last 24 hours of extreme suffering.

Not that I lacked in sorrow. I was joyful in her triumph of saintly life, but we had been inseparable from the first date; had lived a biblical marriage for 48 years. Two had become as one and half of me was leaving.

But there also is loss due to a living death of sorts which in some ways is worse. My elder daughter rebelled at the end of high school as previously discussed: turned her back on most of the family, God, education and a lot more. On the plus side, as finally she matured, she did marry and apparently has been faithful to her husband. They seem to be happy in their secular relationship.

Now twenty some years later, we have a limited telephone relationship. She is pleasant as can be, so long as we are joking around, but at the slightest hint that I want to talk on *any* important topic *whatever*, I hear, "Well, I gotta go." Click. There is only limited communication between us, only artificial humor.

For Personal Reflection and Group Sharing

- Can you tell about or write about your experience of the loss of beloved family and friends?

- You might write a letter to each one, telling them of your gratitude for their loving ways. Send it "virtually" in prayer. You might find

you are hearing in your heart words
back from them.

Being Ignored by Younger Adults

"Do not disregard what older people say, because they too have learnt from their parents" (Sirach 8:9); *"Attend the meetings with older people. Is there one who is wise? Spend time with him"* (Sirach 6:34); for *"wisdom is becoming to the elderly"* (Sirach 25:5).

by Ronda

As a professor of philosophy for some 50 years, I always was teaching younger adults! That usually was true in workshops and retreats where I often was the oldest.

When I retired from teaching at Holy Apostles College and Seminary on campus, I said this to the students on the last day: "Today is the last time anyone ever will have to obey me!"

They laughed.

In social situations, and especially in families where I am the oldest except for my twin who is 20 minutes older than I, these younger adults don't have to obey me.

But I am used to being obeyed by those I talk to. Students have to obey or they won't get good grades. They don't have to agree, but they can't just ignore my wisdom!

So, it was something of a crisis when I emerged at 79 into the world of the retired. Even doing some little group teachings, these participants can just drop out without even letting me know. They certainly don't feel obligated to think I am right!

Adult children? Interestingly enough, the two twin daughters who are still alive have become more interested, occasionally, in my thoughts, than they were when they were in their 40's and I was 60.

Hindsight, I understand this. Even if they had stayed in the sacraments of the Church, they could have chartered their own pathways by becoming, say, liberation theology Catholics vs. my kind of magisterial Catholics.

However, there were key moments when each of them listened to me big time. I want to tell you about them to give you hope if you feel miserable because your adult children don't follow your great advice.

I was visiting my daughter in California. She started talking about the past. I thought that, because I am a well-known figure in the Church, she felt she had not succeeded.

"Diana, the wonderful qualities of your personality, your warmth of heart, joy of life, and incredible generosity, are much more important than any achievements in the professional world."

Tears in her eyes, she asked me to sing with her the "Salve Regina" – the hymn we sung together when she was a child before bed each night.

The other daughter, Carla, is in North Carolina. At age 50, diagnosed with lymphoma cancer, and in great pain in spite of medicines, this daughter began to see the face of Jesus visibly comforting her and heard his voice audibly speaking to her. She started a prayer group on line for family and friends to pray for her to be healed. To my surprise, the format is similar to that of prayer groups I used to run that she hated when she was a teen!

Now with grandchildren it is quite different. They usually don't have a need to rebel against grandparents. As one pundit explained, grandchildren and grandparents get along so well because they have a common enemy! Most of them went with me to Church at one time or another when I was living in their homes. Some are still sacramental Catholics, some are not, but they all listened to many things I said with attention and sometimes read my books.

Now, at age 80, I find I have a new audience! A family I know here in Corpus Christi is home-schooling their children. They asked me if I would tutor the older ones, 10 and 12 years old, in an introduction to philosophy. How I loved simplifying my book on that subject by using examples from their own daily lives as witnessed by me on visits.

My prayer is this: Holy Spirit, keep me from despairing because beloved family and friends, mostly are not my disciples. Open me to humbly teach as opportunity arises. Someday may we all be together forever in your heavenly kingdom.

by Al

First, let's look at this problem from the perspective and understanding of younger adults. Today's young adults are:

1. Working outside the home; men and most women alike.
2. If married, the couple is likely to be raising children.
3. Many are working in distant cities, commuting home on weekends.
4. To get ahead, many mid- and high-level jobs require attendance at company social functions after working hours.
5. For the sake of production and profit, companies are demanding workers to "multi-task"; i.e., work on several tasks at the same time, often on overtime.
6. If they have any time at all to themselves, they likely will want to explore their relative newness of life from their own age perspective: time off with their spouse and children in their own place and with friends, trips, and the like.

And more, besides. In other words, most young adults are harried and have little time to reflect on life or (as St. Paul suggests) to *anticipate the needs of others*. So, what is the elder supposed to do to attract the attention of the younger adult?

If you are still mobile, *anticipate the needs of others!*

The young adults of your family could use a little help – a lot of help! But offer gently; and show no offense if an offer is declined. There is a difference between persistence and nagging. Know when to back off.

Or, recall the constant need of charitable organizations for help. Volunteer according to your life experiences and help the poor, the lonely (which will include some adults younger than yourself), the more elderly, the incarcerated and the homeless. Include incarcerated and homeless teens. Or organize and lead a prayer group, or a Bible study, join a church or social group or teach cooking, or quilting or whatever hobby you have been involved in: be an active, contributing member. An elder friend on the Florida coast used to teach the construction of crab and shrimp traps.

Some other examples: my wife visited and taught the faith to homeless street kids and teens in jail. She carried meals to dying HIV patients in their homes. She visited the more elderly who were house bound or in elder care facilities. She taught CCD (religion) at our parish. She made quilts and gave them to chronically sick women and for sale at school fund drives.

If you have sufficient income, remember charity organizations of your choice.

Remember your young years and the arts or projects you wanted to engage, but never got around to. As for me, I write. I exercise my training in pastoral counseling and spiritual direction informally at the drop of a hat. I play bridge twice a week with 15 to 19 other folks, and I just joined a weekly meeting group, for whom

I will be giving talks on a host of different topics.

Here is an extreme, but actual example. Some 20 years ago, three elderly women in Paso Robles, CA, dreamed of starting a Marian Eucharist Conference in their small ranch and vineyard town. They brought up the idea in public and were told they were too old to accomplish such a complex project. That was all they needed to hear.

They went to work and established a first-class conference that attracted National speakers the first year. The conference attracted 300 attendees the first year and 500 or more each year to their little one-horse town. Most in the crowds were much younger than the three founders. We attended years 1, 2, 3, and 5 before we left for Texas. They and their conference were the talk of central coast California Catholics. "Impossible projects only take a little longer!"

If you are homebound: modern technology allows you to reach out and touch someone. Internet! And that is the way the younger communicate, anyway.

If you are critically ill or infirmed or disabled, there are organizations dedicated to the aid of your infirmity. They will have specialized ideas to match your specialized condition.

There is absolutely no excuse for "woe is me" despair! There are younger adults out there looking for and dedicated to helping people with your condition. And not all of them are looking for monetary compensation. Take action and control your life within your limits to the very end.

For Personal Reflection and Group Sharing

- Are there any people younger than you who listen with interest?

- What are things you enjoy doing that also can be done in groups?

Anxiety about Living Situations Now and Later

"If you wait for perfect conditions, you will never get anything done."
(Ecclesiastes 11:4)

by Ronda

Way before I turned 80, I started trying to devise ideal living situations for me in my old age. How wonderful it would be if someone with administrative gifts would figure out how to turn an old convent or retreat center into a retirement home for creative Catholics. Instead of watching re-runs on TV all day, we could have one evening for Catholic poetry reading; one for sacred music...one for Scrabble – the only board game I ever won!

One of the men I worked on the most to bring about this scheme, a retired businessman, finally said "Look, Ronda, every utopia becomes a gulag!" He didn't add "Especially if you, Ronda, are the leader," but I was sure he meant it. If you don't know what a gulag is, it was the name for the prison camps in the Soviet Union!

Talking to other "oldies but goodies" as I call my friends of my age group, I find that all of them spend lots of time pondering such possibilities as these:

Live with my adult children:

- Pros - They love me. I love them. I can influence the whole family for the good.
- Cons – Their lifestyles are so different, it would drive me nuts to live with them; I would be a terrible burden; if not financially, then

emotionally; they need to have
their own lives.

Here is a poem I wrote about this
option:

81-year-old Hag's Song

Flee, flee, flee,
to the bosom
of the family;
to the bosom of those
who without me wouldn't be?

Where plentiful delicious
food and drink
there be,
and, also, tender care of
me!!

But bosom rhymes
a bit with thumb!
Under whose thumbs
Do I really want to be?

Ah, take the joy,
the pain,
the love,
and,
eventually,
I, Jesus,
will take you
to the Trinity!

A possibility considered by some singles, and some widows/widowers or divorced, is living together with another person of similar age, not in the family. Even at age 80. The plan may be to be friends, like roommates, or to have a sexual relationship, with or without marriage. Of course, having sex outside of marriage is understood to be morally wrong for many reasons. (See my book *The Way of Love*, the section called "Making Loving Moral Decisions")

Depending on what variation of living with friends is being envisaged, there are many pros and cons that need to be considered:

- Pro: Less loneliness, more company, and/or the joys of physical intimacy.
- Cons: Someone could want to live with us to exploit us financially under any arrangement. This possibility could be masked by declarations of great friendship or spousal love.

A person who is highly compatible as a friend may be very incompatible in daily life. Those who treasure quiet don't do well with others who are noisy, especially because of loud TV, Internet videos, or music. Those who love neatness do badly with those who like lots of things around them, sometimes in a cluttered fashion. You, the reader, easily could add to this list of conflicts from your whole past life. Sometimes the couple is compatible, but the families of one or both who visit often may disturb the roommate.

A remedy for the negatives, retaining some of the positives, is have some very, very, close friends nearby in a separate dwelling. These can share their daily lives on a frequent basis, providing empathy, warmth, and fun.

Another option is going into assisted living, followed by a convalescent home, followed by, if necessary, the dementia wing.

- Pros: Not being a burden to family; hopefully good care, plenty of company, daily Mass if it is a Catholic institution, rosary together with others.
- Cons: In my case, some of these have costs greater than my income which is made up of social security and a pension. Medicare would pay for the convalescent home, but I have no ailments severe enough to qualify. I am told that some such residences are very badly run.

Being with only the elderly could be depressing. I find that I love seeing little children around at Church and in my present apartment complex.

Sometimes God answers our prayers virtually vs. literally. As I gaze at the daily communicants in our small parish, most of whom are elderly, and some, who are assisted in getting rides to the Church, I often think "Here is your assisted living community, Ronda!" Over time there is a spiritual bond between the "dailies" even if we don't see one another in our homes.

Living alone very simply with help is another option. I have tried this for 2 years since retiring from living in a dorm as a professor at a seminary.

- Pros: Lots of peace and quiet. Having my own rhythm. A feeling that Jesus, my best friend, is here with me.
- Cons: Loneliness! Even though I have wonderful, very wonderful, friends, including Al Hughes, my

co-author, that still leaves many, many, hours of being alone. Bringing in a cat helped, but not so much. I don't really like my usual company being me, myself, and I! It leads to brooding, anxiety, and convoluted thoughts, inspired by evil spirits!

Now the big news is that I have decided I am too old to live alone. When I started living alone a year and a half ago, I had the fantasy that living alone would mean so much more time for prayer that I would be levitating on the ceiling. Instead, I just feel lonely. But also, my spiritual director agrees that it often is good for 80 plus people to be with family.

My refuge place will be my grand-daughter Jenny's new house rental in Hot Springs, Arkansas, where her husband, Sean, just got a job teaching geology. They are renting a house that has a mother-in-law suite. So, in exchange for a big chunk of my pension and social security, they will get me to daily Mass. Since they are daily communicants, this is not too hard! Keep my quarters at 78 degrees and feed me delicious gourmet healthy meals. I will do the dishes, baby-sit, and pray constantly, plus, of course, utter sage sayings 12 hours a day! Go to goodbooksmedia.com and click on Still a Catholic and read their miraculous story of Sean Hurt's conversion and Jenny's reversion to the Catholic faith.

Those of you who know me personally know that I am not the easiest person to live with, so you could pray that Jenny and Sean will be able to stand me in spite of personality conflicts. Hopefully the mother-in-law suite will be a help for all.

Now, here is one of my fantasies for this time living with my granddaughter and family. Suppose that without my usual book-writing, teaching, and workshop projects, I mostly will be trying to be an instrument of love, responding lovingly to everything that presents itself? PRAY FOR ME!!!!!

Meanwhile, in prayer, Jesus seems to tell me that it doesn't matter where I live now. What matters is that I let Him draw closer to my heart so that He can prepare me for eternal life. Just hold My hand tighter.

by Al

Ronda, I thought, had covered it all on this topic with her pro and con format. I told her I did not think I could write on this subject. Because I, a professional long-range planner with the Air Force and Federal Services Corp. had already planned my own future in great detail with a logical approach.

She said, "Write about that! They need to understand the many issues that readers will have to consider as they make their own plans." We decided that I might use a laundry-list format of sorts.

What Now?

I know better than to say no to a Ronda-matic planner and schemer. So here goes.

I am 78 and see only two more moves remaining in my life; a possible move to an elder-refuge and a later move to a cemetery. But for now, I'm not going anywhere except for a few trips each year. *Because*: I like it here. I like it here because (here comes my first list of issues which you also should consider if you are thinking of moving):

---

1. When I was very young, riding shotgun down a palm lined boulevard in New Orleans, I decided I wanted to live where there were palm trees. Later, during my ocean sailing days, I decided that I wanted to live where there was a world class yacht basin right down town. Tah-daaah! Corpus Christi has both. I live in a reasonably priced luxury loft just a two-block

walk from the yacht basin and have five palm trees just outside my window; more of them all over town. What were your dreams for an elderly place of domicile? Do those dreams still apply?

2. My church is led by the most competent, magisterial, hard-working, visionary priest I have ever known. And he is my personal friend as well. I am not leaving his parish on anything less than a last ride to the cemetery. Do you have an excellent spiritual guide at hand?

3. I have a circle of bridge playing friends mostly in their seventies to nineties. One of them is a 97- year-old WWII Navy fighter pilot. His vivacious wife, age 91, was a WWII telephone operator. All of us appreciate each other's history and stories. (The young seldom can relate.) Do you have a circle of friends from the same or a close

generation? It takes years to re-establish a network of friends in a new place. The older you are, the harder it is to gain a new network!

4. Right now, I am in perfect health. I have a cardiologist who calls me his star patient and a world class heart surgeon who took care of my plumbing problems with a quad-bypass and a carotid artery rotor rooter. Both just a short drive away. Do you have good medical specialists near at hand?

5. Retired of the Air Force, I have a Navy air base just down the beach a few miles. I love jet noise - the sound of freedom! Do you have the satisfaction of your historic druthers where you live?

6. Yes, it is hot here July through mid-September. But from October through March the weather is great, attracting thousands of winter Texans. They love the place seasonally and so do I. I try to tra-

vel to coastal Florida and California between August and October. Are you able to travel? Are there seasonal issues to consider, such as wind/rainstorm seasons? Frequent tornadoes? Earthquakes? Either where you are or where you think you might go.

7. I have no in-house relative who out of the goodness of heart keeps trying to organize my life and tell me what to do. Most people I know want to avoid that as long as possible. So: I desire to remain independent as long as possible.

On the other hand, sooner or later genetics and time will catch up to me. Plan B is my younger daughter. She lives in southern California; has been asking me to move in with her for several years; but understands my attachment to Corpus Christi. There are a few pluses and minuses to consider:

1. California has the highest taxes in the country. That was why I left there in the first place. Two retirement checks and still, I slowly was going bankrupt! I loathe feeding the state government's political lusts for power and wealth on the backs of the citizenry. If you decide to move, beware of tax, political, religious and social issues in your projected new place that may cause you stress.

2. On the plus side, the west coast has one of the best rail passenger systems in the country. From San Diego to Seattle and Vancouver, you can get where you are going in a jiffy. And Seattle has a Nationally awarded bus service that can't be beat. Before you move anywhere, consider the availability of transportation. Especially, if you no longer drive.

3. My southern California daughter is as much a professional and social friend as a relative. Her own circle of friends are like her. I have met them

and love them all. When absolutely necessary, that is where you will find me. But I will be buried with my wife in Corpus Christi, the Body of Christ.

4. My final message on an elder-move? Don't be too quick to leap. As you seek your elder-paradise, first consider where you are. Change can be hard and irreversible.

One more comment. Ronda mentioned the practice of elders living together, married or not, in a sexual relationship. Marriage of the elderly can work; I have happy friends who have chosen that option. But a sexual relationship without marriage is forbidden by Christ, by right reason and by long Catholic Tradition. It is not just about sexual drive; co-habitation in marriage is about life-long commitment, one to another.

In today's sex driven culture, sex seems to be the only decision factor; but true love is about commitment – sex must be a secondary factor; an expression of commitment. Sex without commitment is selfish gratification at any age, not an expression of love for another. Without legitimate marriage, when the sex runs out, someone likely is going to be abandoned deep in their elder years.

As a final issue, many people over 80 are looking for help should they become disabled. So long as sex is not in the picture, mutual help and even living in the same dwelling may be preferred to the strictures of actual marriage.

Here is my approach to the subject of elder-marriage. The Catholic Catechism gives three and only three reasons for marriage: procreation of children, education of the children, and the good of the couple. The first two are non-starters for the elderly. The third reason remains, all important. In a particular question of marriage, what is the meaning of "the good of a *specific* couple"? Are they considering the proposed marriage for true, committed love? For tax purposes?

Only for sex? To escape a bad situation, including disability? Has the couple considered the inherent loss of certain freedoms implied by marriage?

For me, if it is not for true love and life-long commitment, elder marriage is a non-starter. It is perfectly appropriate to have all the benefits and freedom of close, other-gender friendships: even celibate love; while remaining free of the obvious burdens of marriage.

For Personal Reflection and Group Sharing:

- Describe your own thoughts about living situations you are in presently, or think about for the future?
- What does Jesus seem to tell you about living situations?

Limitations of the
80-year-old

"Even to your old age I will be the same, And even to your graying years I will bear you! I have done it, and I will carry you; And I will bear you and I will deliver you." (Isaiah 46:4)

by Ronda

Forgetfulness.

Way before becoming an 80-year-old, I began to forget more often than whatever I considered normal at, say, 40 years old. I recall laughing when a 70-year-old friend started calling his memory his forget-ery!

There can be quite a long period between being averagely competent and being technically demented! Each new type of senior moment can be startling.

My worst was walking out of my dorm room at the seminary with a poncho not covering my jumper, but only my slip! (A man who is only 60 who read this sentence admitted that he didn't even know what a slip was.) Well, most 80-year-olds know that women who still wear dresses, like to wear a silky undergarment so that their legs don't show through their dresses!

It was Thanksgiving weekend and lots of priests and seminarians were gone, but I was horrified that someone might have seen me in my slip. I asked a priest I met later that day if I should quit immediately so as not to give scandal. He laughed! "Ronda, most of us old priests worry that we forget to zip our flies coming out of the bathroom! See if you do it again with the slip and no dress or jumper before quitting."

At 81, living alone in an apartment, I found that I turned on the faucet to fill up the large kitchen sink – walked away – came back 15 minutes later to find the water was flooding the kitchen floor. (It was an old apartment complex constructed before they put holes in the sinks that drain out any overflow.)

A friend of mine, close to 80 years old, tells me the worst thing is losing items in her purse. She bought a purse with pockets for different items, but still she has a hard time.

A related aspect of limitations coming from memory loss is the question of volunteering and old age. It can seem like a good idea; but watch out. I thought it would be ideal to volunteer a few mornings a week at the parish office where there was a great need. The parish administrator is a marvelous woman, patient, and diplomatic, who loves serving the parishioners who call on the phone or come to the window for help with Mass intentions; buying candles, getting sacramental certificates.

Things, which you would think a woman who worked her way through college as a secretary could easily do in a parish office, I found very hard. I can't remember numbers at age 82. So, I put on the receipt for the Mass intentions 2012 instead of 2019!!! Or, I put the god-mother in the place on the certificate that says birth mother.

Humiliating mistakes!!!!

The thing I enjoyed the most, contrary to all expectations, was shredding!!!! I had never even seen a shredder except on TV! I loved the rhythm of it and the sense of closure!!!!

So, after some months of trying my hardest I am now only an emergency volunteer!

Another woman who has been teaching catechetics for 45 years finds that now she is thinking of giving it up. She has trouble with all the equipment needed for the task.

Other Limitations:

Pet Peeve!

I have come to hate the word "just." Not, of course, when it is about justice, but in the slangy perpetual form of:

"Now, Ronda, it's simple....JUST click on this, followed by that, followed by that, followed by that...and you will arrive at your goal on your nifty computer."

Yeah, sure! I added up 10 steps, most of which include references to things on the screen I have never touched, ever, ever, ever, and you pretend this is simple!!!!

"Now, Ronda, JUST follow the directions on the can; it's simple."

Yeah, sure! The directions are in tiny unreadable print. With my old weak hands, I can't push down hard enough to release the top of the can."

"Now, Ronda, to take a cat on the airplane isn't that hard. JUST get sleeping meds for the cat from the vet and put the cat in a carrier."

Yeah, sure! I don't drive. So, to get to the vet I have to ask one of my wonderful, benevolent volunteer drivers to waste a whole morning taking me to the vet, and then, since cats don't have Medicare, paying a fee just to get a tiny jar of liquid sleeping meds...and then try to keep the cat still while holding open its fierce jaws, to pour these meds down her throat...and try to fit me, my carry-on-bag, and the cat carrier into a wheel chair where sometimes the wheel-chair attendants JUST don't show up..."

The rage at how knowledgeable practical people, younger people, try to cajole me into accepting impossible tasks leads, of course, to Confession once a week for yelling at the very dear people who are trying to help me!

Deep sigh!

However, a trick I use on myself when I feel stymied at some simple task I think I can't do is this: "Ronda, if someone gave you $500 to figure this out, wouldn't you figure it out?"

Fragility

I think a lot about types of fragility!

Everyone realizes that if they make it to their '70's and, then, '80's, they are going to be weaker.

My surprise, is that I am not weaker in some ways, but I am fragile in ways I never expected.

I can walk fast on the street, but I can't stand up without wobbling, unless I use a cane.

I can talk loud.

I can still type (though with many typos), and read even faster than before, and do certain puzzles – I just tear out and throw away any puzzle I am not good at; especially what are called Logic puzzles that have nothing to do with philosophical logic about the relation-ship among statements concerning truth.

But, the fragility is different and unexpected. It is a tremulous feeling inside my body or my head when I don't feel competent and strong, but stupid, silly, and weak! This is, of course, com-pounded by senior moments at a rate of 5 a day.

I hate this feeling! I don't notice it when I am doing something well such as talking, reading, or doing puzzles; but, since I live alone, these activities don't take up my whole day!

I try to pray in words such as these: "Dear Jesus, if the only way I will become truly humble and meek is by means of such fragility, let it be."

Obsessing

One of the things I notice, since retirement, is that having much more time, I also obsess about trifles, much, much, much more.

Remedies include these:

Deliverance prayer such as "I rebuke the spirit of excessive anxiety about whether to sweep the floor, or check the web news, and lay it at your feet, dear Jesus, take it away."

Or, with more important but relatively trifling things: "I surrender to you, Jesus, my future on earth, whether it be lived in this place or another place."

Jesus tells me to stop dog paddling in the waves of life and let Him float me to the shore of eternity.

And, that what counts at this time of life is not what I do each day, or plan for tomorrow on earth, but only to be closer to Him, so I can be a greater instrument of love to everyone I encounter.

Fear of Total Disability, Dementia/ Alzheimer's.

I find variety in what each 80 plus person I know fears in the way of total disability. For some, the idea of having to be in a wheelchair is unbearable. But for sedentary characters like myself, there is no fear attached to that at all.

However, the idea of any amount of chronic pain is unbearable. I would certainly prefer to be in a coma from pain-pills than suffer pain above 5 out of 10 and up.

My mother had dementia. I had other relatives who had Alzheimer's and so I am anxious about these. Since Al had years of experience with his wife's

Alzheimer's, I will leave it to him to write about this subject.

by Al

Again, I thought Ronda had "covered the waterfront." But she heard me complaining about a couple of things and said, "Write about that!" And, once again, I know better than to deny Ronda, the writer-matic! So here goes.

I was complaining that I cannot, or should not, be sailing. I still could pilot along-shore, navigate at sea (with a little procedure refreshment), hold a true course, trim sails, crank a sheet winch; and I remember the "rules of the road" when encountering other vessels, on day or midnight watch. All this I could accomplish from the safety of the cockpit. But I dare not go up on deck when underway to tend, raise, reef, lower or secure sails in a whole sail breeze while pounding to windward. Sea legs or not, a fall at my age could lead to broken bones and an early demise. It was different when I was 26, being thrown up in the air above the bow of a 45-foot sailing yacht plowing to windward through six-foot seas.

And of course, no boat owner invites me for cockpit duty. They want and need the help of young sailors who can run around the deck with aplomb while they, the owners, handle cockpit chores.

Do you have a favorite, but risky physical activity you need to set aside?

Also, I have had a burning desire to re-engage motorcycle ownership. I could do it with the three-wheel cycles on the market (less chance of broken bones) or with the new three-wheel car produced by Polaris – the Slingshot!

Wonderful! Exciting to look at and there are half a dozen or more Slingshots running around the streets of Corpus Christi teasing me! But no rag top; no top at all. And I am susceptible to little skin cancers, especially around my face (all due to too much sailing in sunny tropical waters without a hat.) At best, I might get a convertible car with a rag top that closes when the sun is out. But the sun is almost always out here! Sigh.

Are you checking with a dermatologist periodically for skin cancers? If you don't, nothing is more limiting than a good case of cancer!

This morning, before writing, I got up out of my easy chair; thought I was going to faint! It certainly was limiting! It happens periodically, but I have found a cure. Try this. When you get up too suddenly, let it pass, then drink a tall glass of water. Maybe more a little later. Dehydration sneaks up on us as we get older. (A glass of beer might help, as well!)

If at all possible, stay off the elevator. A sedentary attitude likely will lead quickly to major limitations. As I tell folks, "Those who sit and rock for two years often don't get a third year." Hardly anything is more limiting than incapacitation and death! I walk as much as I can, climb the stairs and even walk up moving escalators. If your legs sting or ache a little at the top of the stairs, that's a good thing. You are restoring muscle tone. Push yourself moderately and you will exercise your heart as well as your legs.

Ronda left it to me to talk about Alzheimer's since my wife died of it. It certainly slowed her down during the five years we were aware of it. It took me a year to get her to the neurologist. Four more years to die. Would she have lived a longer productive life if she had gone to him on my first suspicion? Can't say for sure, but if you or one who knows you well suspects any loss of mental function, check in with a neurologist *toute suite*! (Right away!) There are meds that will slow the deterioration of mental function.

Also, there are many forms of dementia. Alzheimer's first attacked her vocabulary access. But it seems it can start with any mental function. Also, in her case, we suspect the end came so quickly that she may have had a complicating stroke. (The neurologist had predicted she would live another ten to fifteen years.)

Finally, there are many books out on the subject and support groups are likely to be available. Reach out and be informed as soon as possible.

For Personal Reflection and Group Sharing:

- What limitations bother you?

- What thoughts and prayers help you accept those limitations?

Capabilities of the 80-year-old

"The just will flourish like the palm-tree, and grow like a Lebanon cedar..., still bearing fruit when they are old, still full of sap, still green, to proclaim that the Lord is just." (Psalm 92: 13, 15-16).

by Ronda

Because there is so much more pain and limitation in life at this time, I find that I get much more joy when I can do anything!

Examples abound. As a child, living in an apartment before washing machines, I used to wash clothes in the kitchen sink and hang them up to dry on a folding wooden frame that could be set in the bathtub.

Now, because it is hard for me to lug laundry to that part of the large apartment house where I live and then go back and forth checking the progress of the clothing in the washer and dryer, I have gone back to washing laundry in the kitchen sink and hanging them on the shower curtain rail in the bathtub.

As I wring out the laundry, piece by piece, I feel ... capable!!! And feeling capable once more is a nice feeling!

Another is the joy of doing different types of puzzles in the magazines like Variety Puzzles, with glances at parts of the solutions in the back of the book. I realize that this gives me, as it were, a cheap feeling of being smart. But also it distracts me from brooding about difficult problems in the world, the Church, and my family. That is because puzzles are really meaningless. I especially enjoy if the solution is some word that is kind of amusing, whose relevance only a person with knowledge of a certain field would think of. For example, the synonym for double-entendre I guessed rightly as innuendo.

It always improves my day if I thank God for little capabilities as in:

"Oh, Jesus, Mary and Joseph, thank you that I brought the garbage out to the bin in the parking lot; thank you that I made lunch; thank you that I put the dishes in the dish-washer."

Sometimes I sing as I go following the lead of Mrs. Doubtfire, of movie fame.

It helps me not to be discouraged by limitations to add up all the things I did do successfully. Okay, I did go around stupidly looking for my phone when it was right in front of me, but I succeeded in going to Holy Mass, cooking and eating meals, cleaning up, etc.

Good feelings also come when I happen to be in the company of other late 70 or 80-year-old's who remember the same popular songs. Sitting at a dining table some associate will begin some silly song, and we start swaying and laughing as we sing. Examples: "100 Bottles of Beer on the Wall," or "Summertime." If you are too young to remember, just google them on your computer or your grandchild's device.

I am still capable of quite intricate conversations with my cat. It is true that they are one-sided but, then, the compensation is I can imagine she always agrees with me.

Sample (while staring into my cat's enigmatic green eyes): "Now, pussy-cat, there is an ontological abyss between you and me, but just the same I can love you, and if you happen to be in a bad mood and scratch me, I stop you but I don't reject you." So, it's the same with God, the Father. There's an ontological abyss between Him and me, but He still loves and forgives me.

I find that God even uses my faults to show me capabilities. I have a nervous habit of peeling cellophane off book covers or peeling off the labels on bottled goods. But this little vice came in handy at the parish. There was a need to peel off labels on old glass candle holders. No one wanted this pesky job but me.

Another capability is just looking at things. When I was a child most old people (anyone over 50 in those days was considered old) would be sitting in rocking chairs on porches. Since I never liked rocking chairs, I didn't think of them as part of my own old age, even when it was upon me.

However, of late, I understand the oldies in the rocking chairs better. Having been a work-a-holic most of my life, I now, as a retired person, when I sit outside my apartment dwelling waiting for rides, find it wonderful just to watch the goings-on around me, such as...

Across the wide ocean front street I live on, a company is fixing up a large house. Every time I am out waiting for my ride I can watch their progress in painting a long wall that guards the mansion from marauders. It seemed as if the adding of new coats of paint would go on forever, but one day it was all done. It looked wonderful.

I like to gaze at the palm trees in the island between lanes on this same street. The first time I saw palm trees when we lived in California I thought they were kind of silly compared to the great oaks of the Eastern country-side. But staring at them now I have come to see the charm of the wide palms blowing in the wind above the thin, thin, trunks.

Watching workers fixing a sea wall that was broken during the recent hurricane, I am fascinated to think what must be in the minds of these tough looking men whose daily tasks are so different than mine were in academe.

Here is one way I described this joy of just looking at things in a blog of mine:

The Secret is in the Sensate

Old, retired people spend a lot of time just looking at things. Having been overly analytic all my long life, it is so restful just to gaze out my window at the palm trees, the birds, and most of all at the ocean.

I was reminded of how the early American theologian John Edwards wrote a whole book to prove that everything in nature is a metaphor to show us what God is like.

So, the sensory holds secrets, as it were.

When I look at a rose I can think – do I unconsciously believe that because God is all powerful, He is hard! Does the rose reveal that God could be soft?

Or, why when I think of Mother Teresa of Calcutta's old wrinkled body do I see it's spiritual beauty, yet shudder to see my own wrinkled body in the mirror? What is God telling me?

A huge remaining capability is reading. I find at this time of life, when I have no obligation to read difficult philosophical books for my classes, that I especially like to read novels, auto-biographies, and biographies about people who lived through WWI and

WWII. It seems to me that I am wanting to take, as it were, a God's eye view of history, before I leave this world.

Of course, many 80-year-old's can still converse. Sometimes dialogues with strangers become humorous: I live right by the Bay in Corpus Christi and our apartment complex has its own fishing pier. An advantage of being an 82- year-old "safe" woman is that you can have cool conversations with men without seeming "frisky."

I was chatting with a 60-year-old fisherman in a desultory way. But since he couldn't avoid noticing my large Benedictine crucifix I asked him if he was a Catholic.

"I'm an atheist. I don't believe in God," he replied smiling.

"Oh, I can prove the existence of God if you like."

"No, I don't."

So, when we got around to chatting about our jobs – he is a surveyor – I said:

"Oh, I was a university professor."

"What did you teach?"

"Philosophy – like proofs for God's existence."

"What? People get paid to prove God's existence????"

by Al

So, I thought I was done with teaching Scripture and Catholic Tradition, organizing retreats, giving talks and even, I considered this to be my last book. But Ronda says we authors *always* think we have written the last one. Like the old war horse, the urge to write pops up at the drop of a hat.

Ronda was reading over my shoulder as I started this section. She got me to thinking, there are some things *only the old* can do well enough to contribute to the wisdom of others around us. A couple of case points:

I found several three-ring binders with all the handouts I used when teaching Scripture and studying spiritual direction. About the same time, I was invited to join "The Friday Morning Group" here in Corpus Christi. This is a group of mostly seniors who gather for a light breakfast, social interaction and for an informative talk.

At the first meeting after joining, the guest speaker did not show up. Afterward, I mentioned to the speaker coordinator that I could give a pop-up talk on several religious topics if it happened again. He consulted the membership, who by acclamation, eagerly approved the presentation of religious topics. (Both Catholics and Protestants present.)

We will be putting several of my topics on the speaker schedule. This old war horse is going back to teaching, not only with the necessary materials, but with the wisdom that comes with age!

The same with spiritual direction. My practice had lapsed for some years. When I began again with Ronda, I was amazed at my ability with that art. Life itself, my natural propensity and the grace of God had continued my training during the lapse. A side factor that helps as well is this. In your 80's people are more receptive to your advice. You are not seen as an intimidating father/mother figure; but are received as a wise old sage. Now I am finding almost daily opportunities to share competent spiritual advice with passing friends and strangers. I am more productive now than in years past! And of course, my last two books, co-authored with Ronda, are reaching out to people I will never know.

The message for you? Consider your past activities and capabilities. Some-where nearby, you can apply the wisdom of your age in volunteer work. Even if housebound, seek out ways to reengage your talents through the internet, or thru in-home discussion groups: such as a knitting circle, Bible study, gardening club, quilting circles, volunteer work, etc.

You may also think of a plan B to implement if mild dementia or forgetfulness gets in your way. For me, I play bridge twice a week. There is a 97-year-old man in the group that is as sharp (though a little slower) as I. Bridge is not only mentally challenging, but a great social opportunity to stay plugged in to local activities and meet younger people.

And a plan C. I always was good at math. So as needed, I will dig out my old analytical geometry/calculus text book and solve differential equations.

You will pick your own plans B and C, etc.

The final message? Stay physically and mentally active to the end of your earthly life. Walk if you can!

For Personal Reflection and Group Sharing:

- Describe to yourself, in writing, or in a group your capabilities.

- Try thanking God for a whole day for what you still can do.

God's Call Now? Am I ready for the Last Journey?

"You have taught me, O God, from my youth, and till the present I proclaim your wondrous deeds. And now that I am old and grey, O God, forsake me not, till I proclaim your strength to every generation that is to come" (Ps 71:17-18).

"You will give me the fullness of joy in your presence, at your right hand happiness forever." (Psalm 46:6)

by Ronda

The title of this chapter came to my co-author, Al Hughes. He believed it came from the Holy Spirit. I do, too!

Those of us, like myself, who love to live in the future by means of over-planning and fantasies of perfect futures, can easily neglect to live in the present in God's presence. Then we fail to hear God's call for right now. Not for the hour of my death, not for purgatory, not for the last year of my life, unless this is my last year.

Right now, I am not on my death bed. It is important in our prayer time to be open to how God wants to grace us to be a better sister or brother to others in the world that surrounds us.

Having written so many books about the spiritual life, I don't want to repeat here, in miniature, everything I wrote. Instead, I want to see what God is teaching me right now.

The most essential call I hear is to become more flexibly open to whatever I encounter each day. Not to keep fighting the reality of the present moment, but to accept the moment as the will of God. To want only to become an "instrument of love" vs. wanting to complete my agenda.

Since I am a retired widow, there is hardly anything except Daily Mass, that has to be done at any given time. Therefore, I can see different encounters not as interruptions, but rather as opportunities, no matter how surprising.

For example, on this particular day I had a merry, friendly conversation with the driver of a Medicare Service that provides me rides to the doctor. Since I dress like a dedicated Catholic with plain clothing and a large crucifix, just that little encounter could have removed some stereo-type my seemingly non-Catholic Christian might have had before.

Or, the diagnosis of the doctor could lead to having to change my whole schedule for the next week, including a trip to another state for a family wedding. My usual reaction would be excessive anxiety about the details of changing plans or not. Jesus is waiting, hoping for me to fling the whole matter into His heart with the new prayer I have been learning called "Jesus, You Take Over."

Or, walking to the adoration chapel near my apartment on the bay, I suddenly notice a spectacular sun-rise. God wants me to slow-down and feast on this glorious sight.

In general, God is calling me away from a work-a-holic life-style into much greater receptivity. I believe this is in preparation for heaven, which is surely much more receptive than daily life on earth.

For many years I have made lists of favorite sayings of spiritual directors, thoughts of the saints and, sometimes, words I think come to me directly from Jesus. I review this list every day during my prayer-time to remind myself of these truths.

As you read my list, you might think, "Does this apply to me, also?" And, at the end of the chapter you could include your own list, whether written down over the years, or only living in your memory.

God alone is enough! (St. Teresa of Avila)

More silence.

Make me an instrument of Your love, Jesus.

Into Your heart I surrender everyone in my family and everyone in the Church I disagree with.

Mary, help me to be sweet and have patience through hope.

Stop trying to control others.

See grace in others.

Don't do anything you don't have to do so as to be more peaceful.

What is God trying to reveal to me this moment?

Don't do and push, but receive and respond.

Upset? Ask Jesus to be present vs. thinking He is only there when I pray to Him.

Together forever with Jesus, closer so He can tell me what to do.

Don't worry about tomorrow. Realistic hope vs. foolish optimism or despairing pessimism.

Be meek. Don't interrupt and override.

Let God do with my family as He pleases, offering my grief and anxiety as a penance for them.

Move and talk *lento*, not *staccato*.

Stay in the present in the Presence.

Stop scheming to avoid suffering, by total acceptance of God's permissive will.

Avoid sarcasm even in thought and replace with kindness.

Kill the ego.

Don't analyze people and incidents so much.

Be a lighthouse, not a captain.

Avoid pessimism by trusting in God.

Depressed? Pray: Jesus I need you right now to keep going.

In agony? Be joyful at the same time, because it is in union with Jesus' sufferings.

With prudence, respond to plans of others for my future.

Don't dog paddle in the waves of life. Let Me, Jesus, float you to the shore, your hand in My pierced hand.

Pray in tongues to avoid too much mental activity.

People, not projects.

Be strong through the Trinity, Mary, angels, saints; not by leaning too much on mentors.

Now I will turn to the last part of this chapter, am I ready for the last journey?

I believe that the best way to be ready for the last journey is to allow God to get much, much, much, closer to me.

Many ardent Catholics like myself already pray about 2 hours minimum a day between Mass, quiet prayer, rosary, mercy chaplet and Scripture reading (in my case the Liturgy of the Hours), and spiritual reading of books by saints and other masters.

So what could bring me closer?

I am finding that it is not so much more prayer as it is praying from the gut rather than in a kind of routine manner. For example, take a repetitive prayer such as "Glory be to the Father, the Son, and the Holy Spirit, as it was in the beginning, is now, and ever shall be." Instead of rattling it off a mile a minute, I could pray it slowly, conscious of the presence of the persons of the Trinity.

Another huge change would be truly bringing every little and big anxious thought to Jesus, begging Him to take care of me as I surrender to His permissive will. Again, not just rattling off such sentiments, but praying them slowly, conscious; that Jesus wants to give me more trust in His personal love for me as His child.

A sure ticket to a long purgatory is having people I haven't truly forgiven. I have done forgiveness exercises often (see especially the one I recommend in *Taming the Lion Within: 5 Steps from Anger to Peace*). If you haven't done such exercises, just google Forgiveness of Others – Catholic Prayers.

So, have I really forgiven others? Since Jesus insists that we will only be forgiven by Him to the extent we forgive others, this question is important.

Forgiveness doesn't mean I have to be ready to spend long periods of time with anyone who is hurtful to me or my family on a regular basis. But it means that when I talk about them to others I don't tell horrible stories about how awful they were to me. And I should hope that they will change, so that if they make overtures to see me, I don't reject them!

You might ask some close friend who she or he thinks are people you haven't forgiven, for instance, judging by your tone of voice when you speak of them.

How about people who haven't forgiven you, especially those whose forgiveness you have never asked for? Is there a gesture you need still to make before you leave this earth?

If they are no longer on this earth, I find it helpful to write a sort of letter to them and then write a supposed answer they might give. This opens the way for a virtual, spiritual reconciliation.

Making it a practice in old age thankfully to affirm everyone you know for all they have meant to you is a blessed thing, always appreciated.

Have you considered making a general confession? What is that, you may ask? It has long been the practice of the Church that Catholics near the end of their journey on earth make such a general confession. It entails making a general list, in your head if not on paper, of the major sins of our life and asking God's pardon once again even if each of these has been confessed before. It is not a detailed description!

Another way to prepare for the final journey is to read up more about the destination. A decade or so ago, my friends Richard Ballard (deacon and theologian), Ruth Ballard (icon-writer) and I wrote a book entitled *What the Saints said about Heaven*. (To find the book, google the title yourself or ask a younger person to do it for you.)

It contains inspiring quotations from the saints about the glories of heaven. At the same time, it refutes some misconceptions that block some believers from longing for heaven. For example, some people think that heaven will only be singing while the angels play harps, or some such. If you didn't happen to like to sing here on earth, this is not too appealing! The saints tell you about other great things we will do in heaven.

Or some think that we become one with God, but never see anyone else we knew on this earth! That has never been Catholic teaching.

Some are so happy about the immortality of the soul that, even though we recite the words in the Creed each Sunday, "I believe in the resurrection of the body," they never imagine what that body will be like! Oh, how magnificent it will be, teaches St. Thomas Aquinas, to have these bodies that are never slow and weighed down, and never in pain, but, instead, soaring!

To be ready for heaven, we should be much more detached from the things of this earth than some of us are. I don't mean going off to a hermitage leaving beloved family and friends. I mean not having closets full of stuff that haven't been used for years! How liberating to realize that those poorer than I could enjoy these possessions for a tiny amount of money at the second-hand shop.

On a practical note, many 80-year-old's I know have pre-paid their funerals and have in the hands of a lawyer all necessary documents involving bequests and pro-life forms of living wills.

Last funny thought of mine – the only way out is up!

This hymn I read recently, says it all!

Hymn from Office of Readings Saturday, 7th Sunday after Easter:

How great the tale, that there should be,
    In God's Son's heart, a place for me!
    That on a sinner's lips like mine
    The cross of Jesus Christ should shine!
    Christ Jesus, bend me to thy will,
    My feet to urge, my griefs to still;
    That e'en my flesh and blood may be
    A temple sanctified to Thee.
    No rest, no calm my soul may win,
    Because my body craves to sin;
    Till thou, dear Lord, thyself impart
    Peace on my head, light in my heart.
    May consecration come from far,
    Soft shining like the evening star.
    My toilsome path make plain to me,
    Until I come to rest in thee.

"Holy Mary, Mother of God, pray for us sinners, now, and at the hour of our death," Amen. We should expect her to be there for us.

---

by Al

It seems that we should not conclude without addressing doubt. Doubt has its positive role and place in our lives. Doubt keeps us sharp, keeps us inquiring, keeps us learning. But if the subject of doubt – however slight – is about God, faith, etc., doubt can lead to worry, anxiety – FEAR! What if there really is no God, etc.?!

In our time, the major cause of doubt is that worrisome argument between faith and reason; church and science. For nearly two hundred years, western society has been fed a choice. You can have faith or reason, but the two are antithetical; you can have one, but not the other!

That is a false dilemma! (A false dilemma is the assertion that you must choose one of two alternatives. It ignores other options, including the option that both may be right. And *that* is closer to the truth!)

We can have both faith and reason. After all, both church and science seek truth, though by different languages and methods. The sciences of astrophysics, cosmology and mathematics now are confirming what theistic philosophers and theologians have known for centuries.

The scientist who has lived by his faith in reason has scaled the mountain of ignorance; he is about to conquer the highest peak; as he pulls himself over the final rock, he is greeted by a band of theologians who have been sitting there for centuries. Robert Jastrow, PhD.

(The details of astronomic and mathematical proof regarding what follows are well beyond the scope of this little book. However, you well may be interested in Spitzer's book, from which we have extracted certain conclusions. It makes for fascinating reading, even if not fully understood. The quotes above and following are from *New Proofs for the Existence of God*, Robert J. Spitzer;

2010, William B. Eerdmans Publishing Company, Grand Rapids, Michigan. Highly recommended!)

Here are the key points:

1. "The Big Bang" is well established as scientific fact. Therefore, there was a creation event and we know that it happened about 13.7 billion years ago. (Also ref. Genesis.)

2. Science now knows that space and time are finite and were created in "The Big Bang". Therefore, neither space nor time are infinite going back into the past. Ideas of infinity are just that, only mathematical ideas without physical reality. (Infinity cannot fit in a finite space.) And, space is not empty; but filled with matter, energy, dark matter and dark energy.

3. Science knows that space-time is expanding and that there will be an end to the universe. Therefore, space time is not infinite going forward, either. *This world is*

passing away. No need to panic!
The end of the universe is trillions
of years hence. That has been
calculated, too!

4. Science has established 20 mathematical constants that govern the
structure and movement within the
universe. All 20 constants are
exactly as they need be to maintain
a stable universe. Change any value
by tiny amounts and the universe
would be unstable; catastrophic to
life.

5. For life of any sort to exist, there
must be a low entropy universe.
(Entropy is a measure of the rate of
expansion or dissipation of matter
or energy. Low entropy equates to
a slowly exploding universe. A high
entropy, fast exploding universe
allows no time for the development
of complex organisms, i.e., life.)

So what?! Based on item 5), with other
established facts, in 1989 Roger Penrose,

PhD was able to calculate the probability of any chance occurrence of a low entropy universe: one chance in a number of tries so large that that number could fill much of the visible universe with 10 font type, if written as an ordinary number, rather than with exponential notation. And of course, chance, itself, does not have being. It is just a mathematical concept with no physical reality. As every philosophy student knows, "from nothing, only nothing comes." Chance itself, cannot create anything.

The "Penrose number" by itself, has caused many of the leading astrophysics/cosmologists to accept the necessary existence of God.

Add to that, the fact that no mindless process could get all 20 physical constants exactly right with such extreme necessary precision. (Item 4, above.)

So here is the conclusion as written by Bruce Gordon, PhD. A conclusion which expresses the opinion of many leading scientists.

When the logical and metaphysical necessity of an efficient cause, the demonstrable absence of a material one, and the proof that there was an absolute beginning to any universe...are all conjoined with the fact that our universe exists and its conditions are fine-tuned immeasurably beyond the capacity of any mindless process, the scientific evidence points inexorably toward transcendent intelligent agency as the most probable, if not the only reasonable explanation.

May we add "Amen?"

One more point, too mathematically advanced to discuss here. *The Physics of Immortality*, 1994, Frank J. Tipler, Doubleday, proports to prove mathematically that God exists and that all humans will be resurrected near the end of time. Tipler is a professor of mathematical physics and a major theoretician in the field of global general relativity.

Graduate students might be able to follow his logic to some point. Recommended for readers highly educated in advanced mathematics.

So, to return to the beginning of this discussion, set doubt and fear aside. God is, we are, and we always shall be.

Do not be afraid. Pope Saint John Paul II, in his inaugural address as Pope.

For Personal Reflection and Group Sharing

- What do you think is unfinished business for you in preparing for eternal life?

- What suggestions of the authors of this chapter could be good for you to try?

- Did any of Al Hughes' quotations from scientists who are convinced of God's existence allay any doubts you have?

Made in United States
North Haven, CT
12 March 2023

33937277R00096